The Asmarians:

The Aliens Who Built the Egyptian Pyramids

The Asmarians:

The Aliens Who Built the Egyptian Pyramids

Horus Michael

The Asmarians:

The Aliens Who Built the Egyptian Pyramids

This book was published in the United States of America. This book is a product of the *Kingdom of Niihau* © ® Horus Michael 2021.

www.amazon.com/author/michaeljcosta

www.amazon.com/author/horusmichael

10 9 8 7 6 5 4 3 2 1 (6"x9")

Genre: Contemporary Science, Occult, Mind/Body/Spirit.

https://www.academia.edu/44103699/Eye_of_the_Pharaoh (**Reference**)

Chapter 1: Asmarians among Us

Asmar is the Ancient Egyptian word for *Emerald*. The only **non-UFO** extra-terrestrials found on Earth are those who incarnate into people via a spirit-like essence of a fiery-emerald light. They are called **Asmarians**. And they were known in Ancient Egypt during the 4th Dynasty.

If you are an Asmarian, you can see (yourself) your emerald light aura when in a completely dark room, like a cave or the inner sanctum of an Egyptian Temple or tomb. Usually this is a rolling emerald-green light, coming from the left eye to the right eye. It may not appear instantly, possibly after an hour of darkness, or near sleep. The aura flares during rest in Outer Space. Astronomers once found them on Mars using telescopes, jokingly asking if they are "little green men?" Green fireballs are known from the Columbus Expedition, and in Native Hawaii as Aumakua. The Prophet Moses found one as the Burning Bush in the Old Testament of the Bible.

Asmarians used Independent life form technology to build the Egyptian Pyramids. This consisted of Geometry and the social organization necessary to construct them. Asmarians can access Dimensional travel via piercing through solid stone to access a chamber in the Great Pyramid of Khufu without opening doors. They use a solid form of themselves (**Asmar crystals**) for this. Each crystal is a 7-sided, opaque, emerald-colored stone with supernatural properties. **It is harder than a diamond and it can cut granite like a diamond cuts glass. It was used to cut the granite blocks in the Pyramid.** Alchemy was developed to create Asmar crystals (**the Philosopher's Stone**). Alchemy meant "The Egyptian."

Cheap tools were left behind on the building site so as to confuse the future people into thinking **wrongly** that those tools built the monuments. The Asmar crystals are still in the Pyramid. Or at least they were once because our people keep remembering this when visiting Egypt. Alexander the Great, Caesar, and even Napoleon knew this, and Napoleon searched the Burial Chamber for the crystals, so he could conquer the World. He didn't find any, or the right kind. He could use them to resurrect or heal his soldiers.

Asmarians can resurrect either themselves or others, and Asmar crystals fashioned into Scarab amulets do this too, as written in the 4th Dynasty, Egypt. Immortality is optional when incarnate.

Asmarians can behave like a Spirit except for their fiery essence which sometimes activates smoke-detectors in bedrooms when nearby. They can **Astral Travel** to Duat or Earth or visit other people. They can fly through Outer Space without a space craft, and can change their outward appearance into shapes, outside of their bodily form. Asmarians are Natural Telepaths and may have other abilities upon discovery.

Asmarians are clones of the Creator Asmarian, Persepone-I, also called PTH or Ptah. The P stands for his name abbreviated, the T is a period, and the H is a double-helix of DNA indicating the Creator (*Master Geneticist*).

Asmar crystals are only operational by Asmarians. The "Emerald on the crown of Lucifer that fell to Earth" is a reference. The crystals may form when materializing into a solid from spirit form.

Asmarians are highly intelligent, talented, or skilled individuals by nature. They are **supernatural** regardless if they yet realize this potential. They seek to be honored or worshiped, and many have discovered Hollywood and the lifestyle of a Celebrity in USA.

Some are drawn to **Egypt** or to the Equator where their powers are magnified by close proximity to the Sun. This is also true of airline travel, and in the **Tropics** or Hawaii.

In Ancient Persia Asmarians were worshiped as "Sacred Fire" in Temples. **In Egypt** the gods Hathor, Ptah, and Osiris are painted **green**, as are plants the First of Creation.

Egyptian Creation "Myths" start with the **Island** rising from the Seas, a reference to the **Asmarian Colony of Atlantis**, their first Earthly home since the Dinosaur era. Atlantis was not a Human civilization, so Humans cannot find it nor know what to look for. **Humans** on Atlantis served as a protein source (*Humen: the Other White Meat*). Their body parts were sold in marketplaces like Chinese Chickens. Atlanteans had different physique than Humans. Ptah invited the others here.

Asmarian Crystals are thought-controlled, as by Telepathy. Humans are **not naturally** Telepathic, so they **develop it** via Prayer or Magic spells. Human people believe that "Atlantis used crystals" so they hoard any type of crystal, not Asmarian type.

Asmarians can also **tamper with Dreams** via *Soul Cube Manipulation.* Every life form has a corresponding white Soul Cube in the Cube Moon near Duat/7D/Nucleus.   The Cubes record all memory that the brain sends there via electric signals. We use it for Judgement after physical death, for "Placement" of Spirits in Duat. We play the Soul Cube and if it doesn't match the testimony of the Soul, then that Soul is deemed a liar and fails the Judgement. In which case the floor opens up and the Soul falls headlong into the Lava below Duat, or is recycled. Asmarians have green Soul Cubes for memory storage only.

Dreams can be manipulated for sending messages to our people during sleep. *Voices* heard by those called "*Mentally Ill*" are from entities **near** Soul Cubes in Duat. It is **not** from Telepathy. Sometimes Soul Cubes radiate thoughts intercepted as vocalizations.

This is **Astral Travel** of the Soul above the body.

The stone blocks in the Great Pyramid were cut so precisely that any thin device could fit between them. This is evidence for **Asmarian Crystals**. No copper tools can duplicate that and expect to work in the amount of time as expressed by Human Scientists. Humans still had to place the blocks in correct order, however mentally controlled. Using such technology is why there are so many Pyramids in Egypt. The layout at Giza resembles Astronomical Constellations. The "air shafts" were there to line up with Constellations at night during construction, and to provide air for workers before its completion. The vaulted chambers are to reduce weight and because of the fear the stones might break.

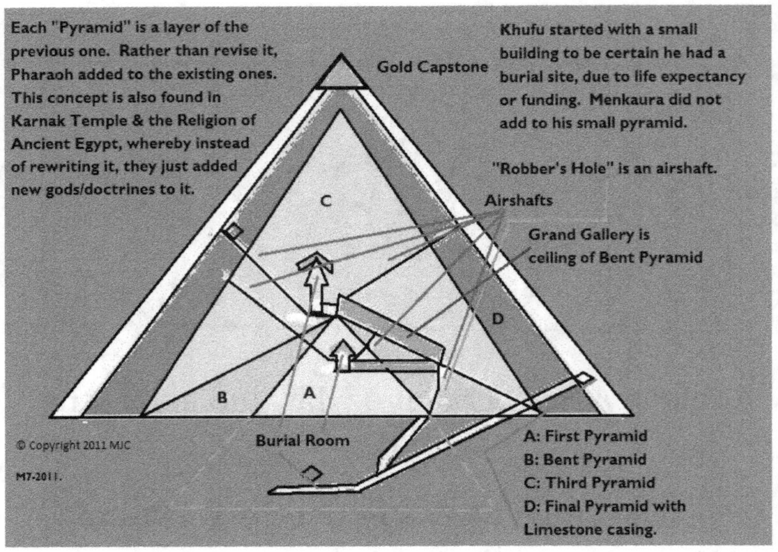

The Great Pyramid was built in about 3 or 4 stages. The first burial room was underground with a sloping pyramid roof. When this was added to, the interior was expanded; the "Queen's chamber" was the next burial room. The next or 3rd phase was expanded so the roof of the 2nd phase became the Grand Gallery of the 3rd phase. The burial chamber here (Kings' chamber) was the last one, with air shafts leading outside. This was clad in white limestone and a golden capstone to reflect Sunlight like a desert beacon. Pharaohs built in stages due to Time, life expectancy, harvest levels, available resources, or amount of workers. Pyramid construction prevented idleness and civil unrest during Flood Season.

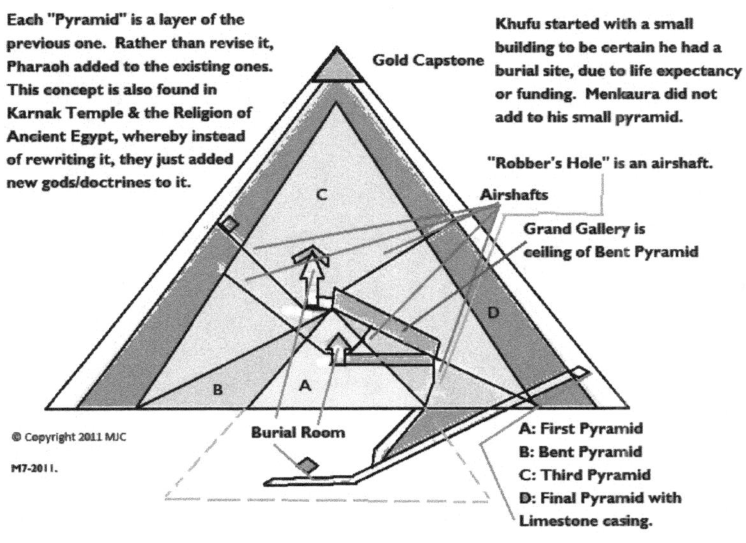

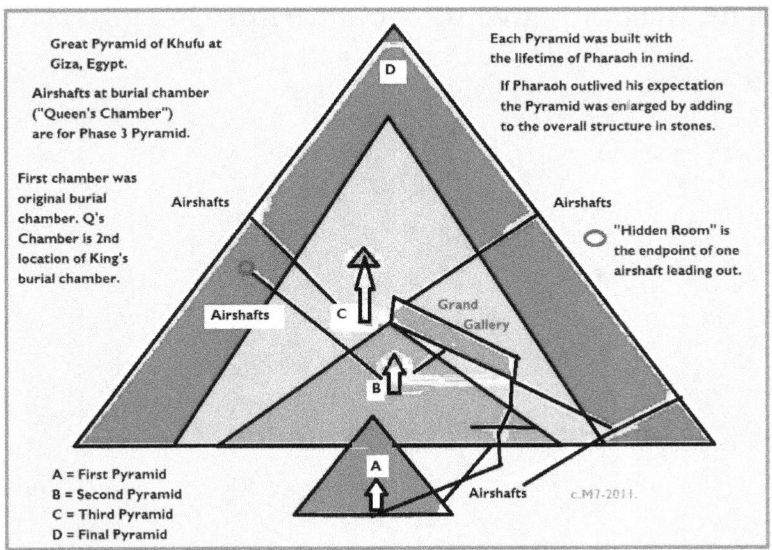

Building the Great Pyramid

The Original "*Eye of the Pharaoh*" ©1990 MJC

Ammot, *the Devourer* (Pet of Osiris)

Chapter 2: Historical Asmarians

Asmarians were first invited by Ptah during the Dinosaur period. An Asmarian named Set (Setesh, Seth or Sutekh) controlled a nearby Planet Achilles, so Ptah thought life on Earth could be neighbors. Ptah was developing Reptilian People as a project after the Dinosaurs.

Ptah invited the others here to help explore the Dinosaurs via incarnation. They did not appreciate him going about chasing or eating the others as a Tyrannosaurus Rex. Most were Herbivores, and a few challenged Ptah's form as a Triceratops. A female Tyrannosaurs (Sakhmet) played with Ptah; she had an interesting tail.

Set's world had Nuclear War, so Set was considered the "God of War" during the Human Era. His Planet exploded while Ptah was watching it away from Earth. Ptah's Planet Earth was hit accidentally by chunks of Planet Achilles. This is now called the **Asteroid Belt**. The ensuing accident killed most of life on Earth, except for birds that could fly away or hide. **Mammals landed on Earth** and eventually overtook the population. Fish still existed, and a few types survived.

Ptah waited millions of years, observing the Mammals or worked in his Celestial Office in Duat (The Nucleus, 7D). He enlisted the other Asmarians as Engineers for building a civilization now called **Atlantis**. It was on an artificial lake on an island **near modern Madeira Island**, just beyond the **Pillars of Hercules** (*these were once positioned to the north and south of the Mediterranean Sea's exit to the Atlantic Ocean*). Madeira was found vacant from people when Portuguese Sailors discovered it. My biological father was born on Madeira, and he told me about this being the remnant of **Atlantis**. The city was built on an artificial lake **like Tenochtitlan of the Aztecs**. The city was designed with interlocking concentric circles with a radius bridge leading out. This was for security mostly.

Atlanteans had different shaped skulls than Humans, some had horns and tails. They were also larger than **Humans**. We call the inferiors that after the Egyptian Gods "Hu" & "Min" – Hu was the God of Taste, and Min the God of Fertility (with an erection); so you are named after an Egyptian expletive. Atlanteans also ate fruit and vegetables as part of their diet.

The City was advanced in technology, similar to Modern Japan. They had small red Jets (flying cars), ceiling retractable showers, carved stone and concrete Palaces, metal and glass exteriors, and industry in the middle circle with farmland on the outer circle. The **Palace of the Nine Princes** existed in the central circle. Boats transported people in between those regions. The lake was of fresh water with some aquatic life. The city was some distance from the beaches. It was about 1 to 2 square miles estimated.

Other colonies of Atlantis existed elsewhere on Earth. Line art was carved from a distance via air ships. These artworks were discovered by Humans after they invented air travel.

The Nine Sovereign Princes (the Ennead) governed Atlantis like a Republic, with the other colonies serving as an Empire. In later years the *Prince of Light* on Atlantis conquered and united the other colonies, but in 3 days he would be crowned sole ruler. On the day before that time, he died while trying to save Atlantis. He was in his Palace when he heard commotion outside. Atlantean artillery fired at the space-tourist UFO ships, which were unarmed. One UFO crashed into the stockpile on Atlantis, and imploded the City.

The end result of the implosion destroyed the City of Atlantis. Other colonies had to fend for themselves. **The UFO ships were unarmed**, but frequently visit Earth. Their home world is overcrowded and they are looking to relocate here. We used Pyramid technology on Atlantis and later Egypt, which came from **their** technology originally. **Pillars are a trademark** of Persepone-I/Ptah. They only existed on worlds of his design.

Persepone-I's laboratory was an underground basement, called Chamber V (5). He experimented with Genetics, **making hybrids** using animal and Human DNA. He stored his creations there until he had a nervous breakdown and had to release them into the wild. These became ideas in later Human Mythology. The hybrids included Vampires, Centaurs, Butterfly people, winged people/Angels, the Sphinx, Unicorns, Pegasus, etc.

One Atlantean Nobleman had a form of **Telepsi** (Audio/Visual Telepathy) where other living people could see/hear him think. He wore headphones that resembled bronze breasts of 2 Amazonian statues that stood behind him like Isis & Nephthys behind the enthroned Osiris. The Current Telepsi works better and has less feedback.

After Atlantis, **Ptah made Egypt his home** for a few thousand years, often returning to visit in his role as Conqueror. He incarnated into royalty so he could govern Humans and compel them to build his projects. Temples, tombs, Pyramids, walls, highway canals attached to the Nile River, Trade Networks, and advances in Human technology are his handiwork. He extended his influence into China, India, Rome, the Americas, and the Incas of Peru. Some ideas are to be found in **Ancient Hawaii**, as in Egyptian Carpentry tools (Adzes), stone Temples, feather robes, Petroglyphs, Mana, and Magic/willed events.

Other Asmarians visited following Ptah's departure or incarnation. The Bible is a synthetic creation. Characters in it want to appear real if they hadn't been taken from Egyptian sources. For one, there are 2 people named Joshua – one as successor to Moses, and the other the Messiah; so the latter was changed into a Greek name Jesus. The word Christ or QRST was Egyptian for "burial." Jesus had a tomb, but wasn't in it when he was baptized. Nor was he in it longer than 3 days. Moses was based on **Ahmoses**, which when read correctly is "Moses-Ah" or Messiah, the **Liberator of Egypt**.

There are **multiple ways** to interpret the Bible's information. Rome didn't like the Egyptians and especially not **Lord Osiris**, the King of Kings who established the First Egyptian State and promised to return in the future to continue his design. This was also promised by the Aztec God-King **Quetzalcoatl**, a "bearded man from the East" (i.e. Egypt). **The Romans created their own version of Osiris, and had him killed by the Roman Government** (so the Roman People could sleep at night). This creation was called **Christianity**, and it was endorsed by Roman Emperor Constantine. So the character Jesus Christ **absorbed** all the titles and attributes from the Osirian religion on purpose, making it appear stolen from Egypt. You won't hear this from believers.

    Another interpretation is that **Set** tried to regain access to Heaven after he was **exiled** from Egypt. Set was exiled for the murder and dismemberment of Lord Osiris, and in later years when people favored the Osirian religion or when it resurged in popularity. His statues were damaged, his temples closed, and offerings went to other Gods. So Set dwelt in Sinai Mountains where he found **Moses**, the Exiled Prince, and indoctrinated him. Set taught Moses **Egyptian Magic**.

The 10 Commandments of Set was anti-Egyptian in nature. Egyptian Pharaohs legally owned everything so they could take what was legally theirs without asking. They also womanized (adultery), and worshiped images of other gods. Set didn't want his people (ISRAEL) to worship other Gods (regardless of Monotheism), or his images because of possible vandalism. Set wanted only meat offerings on an Earthen Altar, as in Egyptian Set worship. Blood offerings were also from Osiris worship, which found its way to the Mayans and Aztecs.

The 10 Plagues of Israel / Set were from Egyptian Magic originally. They can be replicated. Set's **Promised Land** was won by **right of conquest**, one of Set's Maxims. Set was an Almighty God, but not too intelligent. In the **Book of Genesis**, Set as God wanted humanity to be controllable by limiting outside influences. The Serpent was blamed every time Adam/Eve sinned against Set. The people could not accept responsibility for their actions. **Be Fruitful and Multiply** meant "be prosperous and expand your business" **not** reproduce all over the Earth. Serpents are sacred animals of Set, as are Donkeys (as Jesus rode into Jerusalem with). Set also controlled Storms & Earthquakes, as Jesus did.

Set was white-skinned with fiery red hair (Western Jesus); his strength was in his hair (Samson). Set, like the Babylonian Demon Tiamat, was stronger but Horus, the heir of Osiris, was more intelligent and like Marduk, was better equipped. Marduk destroyed Tiamat in Babylonian stories, just as Horus vanquished Set in Egypt. The **Law Code** written by King Hammurabi of Babylon was attributed to Lord Marduk, **not the first** attrition to a Deity. The Egyptian word for Babylon was "ARAM" and the word for the people of Abraham was originally "ABRAM." The Egyptian **Joseph**, whom in the Bible was bought as a slave to Egypt, was based upon **Amonhotep the Son of Hapu**, the Vizier and Seer, because both Joseph and Amonhotep died at 110 years of age. This was during the reign of Pharaoh Amonhotep Nebmaatra of the 18th Dynasty, Egypt.

The son of Nebmaatra was the infamous **Akhenaton**, the First Monotheist/Heretic, and the first Egyptian King to use the title of Great House/**Pharaoh**. He built his new City of the Sun with **forced child labor** (the Children of God). These children may be the Hebrews of the Bible. One of his Viziers was Aper-El, a Hebrew name. The Bible is off by a factor of 10X in recorded events.

Akhenaton ruled 17 years. His heirs ruled maybe 2 years, followed by King Tutankhamon's 9 to 10 years, then Ay's 3 or 4 years. Horemhab ruled 28 years. This is about 61 years. If the Hebrews were **captives for 40 years instead of 400** (if 400 this was well *after* Ramses the Great in the next Dynasty), the **Exodus** was during **Horemhab's reign**. Horemhab died without a child heir, so he appointed his General Pramessu (Ramses 1). **Horemhab then persecuted the family of Akhenaton on their monuments, as they were part of the People of Israel.** There is no evidence that Habiru were conquered or enslaved as POWs (Prisoners of War), the probability is that **they voluntarily became Temple Slaves**, and later forgot why and for how long. **Merenptah**, a son and heir of Ramses the Great, **conquered "Israel"** on his military stele, so they must have **existed prior to the 19ᵗʰ Dynasty**. Horemhab was the last King of the 18ᵗʰ Dynasty.

Tutankhamon was the influence for Moses because he specialized in Egyptian Magic. His Horus name is "Ka Nakht, Tut Mesu" – the Ka Nakht was in his ancestor's titles, but **Tut-Mesu** could be a reference to Moses as Mesu (both mean "born of"); *Born of the Image of the Mighty Bull.*

Both King Sety and Ramses the Great worshiped **Set** in the 19th Dynasty. **Tutankhamon** spent a majority of his time and expense repairing the damages done by Akhenaton's people. He was buried as Osiris in his tomb, but was it his tomb or someone else's? Valley of the Kings Tomb # 62 or KV62 was where Tutankhamon's remains were discovered in 1922 by English Archaeologist Howard Carter. KV62 was Smenkhkara's burial, until it was violated after Tut was crowned, so Tut moved him into KV55 with Queen Tiye. The reconstructed face of the KV55 Mummy matches the face on the 2nd coffin of Tutankhamon, which is not Tut's face and belonged to someone else. Nor does it resemble Akhenaton. Both coffins (KV55 Mummy and KV62's second coffin) had rishi feather design on the exterior. The second coffin did not fit into the Tutankhamon coffins, so one was shortened. The KV55 Mummy is male, once thought to be Akhenaton, and because of a Genetic test that said "**KV55 Mummy** is a son of Amonhotep Nebmaatra and the Father/**Brother of Tutankhamon**." It was too young to be Tut's biological father until after some doctored evidence took place to force this decision. As a brother it proved Tut's father is Nebmaatra, as he said on his monuments.

Chapter 3: Eye of the Pharaoh

The original book was published (stolen first edition) after 1991 or in 1992 by a Psychology Therapist of the Author, **without his knowledge or permission**. The book was Science Fiction and biographical in nature, the Publisher sold it as a "true story" **or religion**. It generated some "$50 Million+ USD" in revenue until the Author alerted the World as to its theft in January 1994 on a pre-Internet BBS (Bulletin Board System) called **SFNET**. The Media all knew about this book and its fallout. Hollywood openly refused to make films based on the book because they said "We don't make movies from terrorists" after they read chapter 20 which had a **fictional war** against Arabic Terrorists; this later influenced the real war on Islamic Terrorism after 2001, as part of the book's prophetic effect. Films like *The Mummy, The Mummy Returns,* and *The Matrix* films **plagiarized parts of the book**. Other people wrongly interpreted the narrator as the "Antichrist" because of two passages saying "my opponent, Jesus" in the story, as the Antichrist is the opponent of Christ in the Bible. They ignore that the **main character liberates** the Middle East to form the Kingdom of God (Osiris) in Chapter 20.

The Therapist did not read Chapter 19 which declared "You wrote this masterpiece of Science Fiction?" with the name of the book "*Eye of the Pharaoh*" asked by a character on a cruise ship to the main character. The main character is the **reincarnation of Tutankhamon**. The story begins to speak about the **Asmarian people** (*Emeraldians*) and about Ancient Egypt, Tutankhamon, and Jesus Christ (*Zorphenal, the Traitor*). The story was **a fictional narrative of the author**, whom is reincarnated Tutankhamon and other Pharaohs, but the story shows what would happen should the author go to Egypt (which he has yet to do as of May 2021). It was written in 1989-1990, when the author was 16+ years old.

Many American Physicists and Astronomers "borrowed ideas" from the book to fuel *their* own theories of topics like Dimensional Physics and Quantum Theory. They believed the author was a **Genius** (as stated by the author in 1994). In 1998 Barbara Walters said on her television show "Barbara Walters Presents" her wanting to interview the author as one of the "most influential people of 1998" as the book's first edition debuted on the International (Black) Market that year, selling from $50,000 each according to the FBI.

Jay Leno of the Tonight Show made a comment about the book once, "You know, now King Tutankhamon can't be a terrorist." The American Psychic Jeane Dixon wrote 2 prophecies about the author – the first was about a vision from 1962 that said the author was the "Messiah" and the 2nd one was more political without historical evidence as "the Antichrist." She said Tutankhamon would rewrite Akhenaton's Monotheist religion, regardless that the **real** Tutankhamon was Polytheist. She did say that the USA Govt. would help advertise the book with their "Widespread Propaganda Machine" (The Internet). The USA did market characters from the book via letterhead from missives by the author during that time, mostly complaints about religion and the book's theft. The author also featured in Political Cartoons in **Newsweek** magazine and in College newspapers, and in Comic Strips in other venues. The **Media** had a meltdown when a leaked passage said "**Justice is revenge**" relating to how the Egyptian god **Horus avenged** his father's death (Osiris) by a court room decision against **Set**. So this featured in a vast number of television shows, movies and in computer games, saying "Justice is not revenge." People do not fact-check now.

The Publisher was studying Psychology in the author's future University and used his family for her Master's degree **research.** He told her about his beliefs in reincarnation and said he wrote a book about it. She was interested and asked to borrow it to read. She returned the book after a few weeks, secretly photocopying it. This was in 1991. By 1992 it was published via a real publishing company. The author discovered this by accident. He heard people talking about it, gossiping and women in his College Algebra classes kept trying to gain his attention by dressing up as a character from his book. One was a girl from Egypt who kept asking for "King Tut." The author twice dressed in the season of Halloween **as an Egyptian Pharaoh**. Some people believed this costume was "evidence of trans-sexual content" because it incorporated an Egyptian Kilt and Cosmetics (as invented by Ancient Egyptians). Later Halloween costumes were generic Egyptian Pharaohs in the year 2000's. When the author attended his University, women kept trying to make him contact them in classes. Women believed the book was a **Romance novel** as relating to Queen Ankhesenamon. One blond woman followed him home and said outside "I love you!" Another stalked him for 17+ years.

At his first College the **on-campus radio station** made a **surprise on-air interview** that the author dismissed as a false phone call. This was *before* the Author knew his book was in circulation in 1993. He thought this was a political call because he was photographed by the College Media newspaper that year when **he dyed his hair midnight black.** His hair was originally red the first year after his birth, and later became darker. He dyed it for cosmetic reasons.

The author was involved in Politics during the 1990s. He convinced the American President Bush (Sr.) to retake Kuwait from the Imperial Ambitions of Iraq. The Liberation of Kuwait was a success. He also used **Egyptian Magic to liberate** the USSR in 1991 and North Korea in 1994 during the Summer Season.

On SFNET the author used the pseudonym "**M7**" to say one night that the author was killed to see if anyone was listening or paying attention. The next day at the University some people were crying, and the CIA set up a person at his bus stop resembling him and his gestures. The CIA classified the book/author "top secret." "M7" later had gossip relating to the proceeds of the book.

In March 10, 2020 the first Publisher of the book died of Brain Cancer. She had a "go fund me" website established for medical costs. In 2018 her house burnt down during Fire Season, eliminating all evidence of the author. The author republished **Eye of the Pharaoh** numerous times, but no one bought it from him. They prefer the illegal, first edition. Even one of his neighbors bought a copy for $50,000 once. The same neighbor's family was in Chapter 18, and they were obsessed with "M7" and the wealth generated by the book. The author has yet to be paid (due to CIA's classification). Rumor has it in the "hundreds of billions," since the original 500M copies resold on the Dark Web.

<u>https://www.academia.edu/44103699/Eye_of_the_Pharaoh</u>

In High School the author was identified as an "Alien" during a religious retreat or class, because he told them "I resurrected once," and they linked his interests of Egyptology and Astronomy together. Later in Biology class the students realized how unique his attributes were, as further evidence. The Publisher was the author's babysitter once, who accidentally walked on him as he slept on her carpeted floor in her residence; he awoke in Duat and later resurrected back on Earth.

The Musician **Michael Jackson** identified with a character from the book (*Akhenaton, or Zorphenal*), and communicated with the author in the 1990s to early 2000s. He is **Asmarian**. The author wrote to MJ's ***Never-land Ranch*** numerous times, trying to coerce MJ to join his cause, which was once on **Saturday Night Live** television show with seven clones of MJ entering a space ship (the Michael Seven/M7). The author once created a music video on Youtube.com following MJ's drug overdose death in 2009. This was later removed when **Sony** Germany (Music Company) complained. The author once suggested building a **Museum** to honor the Musician at *Never-land Ranch*.

One modern Superhero is **The Green Lantern**, originally inspired by the Aladdin's Lamp story in Arabic literature. This Superhero **uses Green Light** to control objects via his thoughts. The Green Lantern is a memory of **Asmarians**.

Many people identified with the story, including a teenager who was in a convertible car that pulled up near the author in traffic, saying: "I don't like being called a Traitor." **Crazy people** mostly identified with the book due to the way the **Publisher** was marketing it.

<u>**Chapter 4: Other Worlds**</u>

Other Planets prior to Ptah being on Earth **were seeded** (life was established) in the Milky Way Galaxy. The majority were Independent Life, mostly **secondary forms** (like Humanoid or standing **upright** and walking on two legs). Most of these are **Positive** in their thinking alignment (non-evil). These life forms later became Angels in Heaven, and appear as "**orbs of light**" in spirit form. Variations use space travel to visit Earth, they also can **Astral Travel** here in spirit form while their distant bodies are asleep. They once told the author (while in Astral Form) that **Humans "are too hostile"** to make contact with and they are waiting for Humanity to change first (*which as you know is nearly impossible*). **So by creating events** of wars, hostility, civil unrest, etc., **that Humanity will eventually change to be more positive**.

One world had a female "**Mermaid**" creature on it; this later inspired the Mermaid of Mythology once remembered while incarnate on Earth. Her people had scaled green tails in place of legs.

Another planet contained two halves of opposing aligned Independent life. One half was pure positive, Primary Forms that "liked licking themselves"; the other half was hostile negative alignment that liked war, and "didn't like licking." The negative forms had spiked heads. Primary life forms are basically spheres with a mouth, the eyes are inside the mouth and can extend when necessary. They move via levitation or via gravity manipulation.

In a Supernova, Ptah once had to confront an **Asmarian** that felt he was dishonest in their relationship, or that he "stopped loving her" when she became evil. This was later cleared up after Ptah entered the Supernova (a dim Star). The Supernova was filled with negative energy.

On one Planet Ptah was organizing Humans for battle and another female **Asmarian** (Sakhmet) decided to interrupt his work and have her new army attack his army. Asmarians use life forms **as toys for their amusement.**

Asmarians are clones of Ptah from the Outer Realm (11D), wherein his body sleeps. The Universe is the Interior Realm, inside his sleeping body. So his Mind controls the Body, inside and out.

In Ancient Egypt, Ptah "creates by his thoughts and divine utterances/speech." So the Universe is the inside of his body, controlled by the Mind which is Ptah.

Originally all the clones were exact likenesses of Ptah's **Asmarian form** (Emerald Light). They gained a physical form **only** from Incarnation into the living. His Asmarian form was cloned but not the body in 11D, which is humanoid in form. Each clone had their Personality altered by percentage of attributes, to make them unique. **When they reproduce in Outer Space** they first ask for the other Asmarian's "secret name" (identity) and then **trade *Personality Components* or attributes**. Such components are like "war, peace, creativity, intellect, artistic, conquest, etc." They are traded like a card game. Their names also came from Incarnation on Planets. He made clones to avoid being alone, and because he could use them to add to the Creation much faster than by himself. He extracted Asmarian "genes" and added this to an Egg placed in the body before detachment and entrance in Spirit form. **Thoth** was the first to leave the Egg, and he immediately started counting (Time), so as to create a Time Tunnel for traveling through events. **Duat** is the Nucleus inside the body.

The origins of the Big Bang Theory as written are when Lord Osiris was killed and dismembered by Set, who scattered the parts of Osiris all across Egypt. These parts represented Stars and Planets; Osiris is Order, and Set is the forces of Chaos personified. At the End Times, Horus (Light) reassembles the bodily parts of Osiris to make him whole; this is the Great Crunch Theory whereby the Universe stops expanding and retracts back together. The BBT was a theory of **Astronomy**.

In actuality the unstable Matter and Antimatter were collected outside the Nucleus, and then detonated from inside Duat. Asmarians collected this energy and activated it. The purpose was to spread Planets and Stars outwards for equal regions. We did this many times, and each time we add perfected Spirits into the Voidal Stream (i.e. a blood vessel that uses transfigured Akhu Spirits as Antibodies), the Void is the area outside the Universe wall. Each Universe is like a cell or organ inside the body in 11D. The organ pumps perfected Spirits into the blood supply. **The purpose of Planets like Earth is to perfect Spirits by Incarnation and Judgement.**

Spirits are the Mind or driver of a body. Each Spirit is perfected **by living** (Incarnation) and by **choices of actions**, which are judged by the Gods after death. This process determines who enters the Body's blood supply in 11D. Only positive Spirits become **Antibodies**, negative ones are other types to limit over-population on Planets. Heaven is a temporary holding cell in Duat where positive Spirits are kept until the Universe contracts and they are sent on their way. **So Ptah incarnates on Planets to maintain this System.** *This is the Purpose of Life.*

<u>**Note:**</u>

The Author *experiences the "fiery emerald light" whenever in complete darkness or near sleep. Only those with this can identify with* **Asmarians**. *It was tested for hallucination, which was* ***negative***.

Chapter 5: The Asmarian Holy Grail

In "*The Templars and the Grail, Knights of the Quest*, © Karen Ralls 2003, the author positively identified the Holy Grail as a Stone that "fell from Heaven," "an **Emerald** that fell from Lucifer's crown during the war in Heaven," the *Lapsit Exillas* or "Stone from Heaven," or meteorite. Volcanic glass of a light green color was found in Tutankhamon's tomb made into a pendant of jewelry. It was from a **meteorite**. This Emerald stone in Rall's book has *healing properties*. This is also called the *Lapis Elixir*, or **the Philosopher's Stone**. The Templars were the descendants of Christ/QRST, a group of Knights devoted to preserving holy relics such as the Ark of the Covenant or the Holy Grail. They are called the Poor Knights of Christ of the Temple of Solomon, or **Knights Templar** for short.

The Stone/Grail can resurrect the dead and heal the sick. This is a description of the **Asmarian Crystals**. The word Crystal has **Cryst** (Christ/QRST) in it. The QRST is the word for *Burial* in Egyptian, a sacred ritualized burial **to identify with Osiris**, as in Tutankhamon's ritualized burial.

Chapter 6: The Nucleus of Duat

The "Barrier Zone" is a word for the Nucleus of each Universe, wherein lays **Duat**, the Other World. Black Holes mostly connect to Duat by gravity, sending their contents there. A Black Hole is like a whirlpool in a bath tub that sends trapped particles into the drain. These form by collapsed Stars that implode, forcing gravity inwards rather than attract objects in orbit. The center of the Milky Way Galaxy has a massive Black Hole: this is what happens when Set stops protecting Ra from Apophis. Apophis is the Lord of Darkness, as in solar or lunar eclipses, the Great Worm, enemy of the solar Gods. **Set** protected the Boat of the Sun from Apophis in his afterlife usually with a **spear.** This spear is the **Holy Spear** or element of the **Grail**. So the spear must be made of **Asmarian Crystals**. This description is repeated by future cultures like St. Michael spearing the Dragon, or St. George spearing the Serpent.

Duat has the **offices** of the Asmarians. The offices were fashioned from Hathor's doll house, recycled for this purpose. Duat is the prime location for the Afterlife Dimension; Heaven, Hell, & Purgatory are locations there.

Heaven is mostly cloudy, having most of its population in snow-capped mountains with trees. These mountains remind one of white limestone-capped **Egyptian Pyramids**. There are fortified cities with golden fences atop granite walls and golden pylon gates. **Angels** (Akhu) are its police/military. People wear silk robes and wrap-around sandals of gilded leather, as on Atlantis. The weather is warm with a slight breeze. People dine on everlasting bread and cakes, beer, wine, pure water, fresh fruits & vegetables, and the *Food of the Gods*, or **Tchefa**.

Hell is pitch-black darkness with no stars or constellations. **Aset Tchabet** (Place of Punishment) is overcast with clouds. Demons chase the Damned in these regions (*I traveled to Duat via Astral Travel during the time when I designed my Egyptian Book of the Dead in 1994-2004 CE, and noticed these places*).

Purgatory is where Souls are forcibly neutralized, **or purged**, as a way to preserve them from punishment after death. People who are involved in Mass Shootings, Arson, riots, vandalism, Terrorism, or other crimes are found in **Hell** & **Aset Tchabet**. Jesus Christ descended into Purgatory after death to be cleansed of the World's Sins he absorbed.

Amenti and the Fields of Reeds or Fields of Offerings is the usual location of Ancient Egyptian people in **Akh** form. Here there are Cities, Pyramids, Temples, the Necropolis where souls enter from, and other regions. **Amenti replicates Earth cities** and regions for souls from that planet. Each replication is pristine or new in appearance, without pollution, crime, or normal weather.

After Judgement in the Court of Ma'at, souls are subject to "**Placement**" where they choose the location, habitation, possessions, pets, businesses, and family or friends in their afterlife. **Good Deeds** performed on Earth equal a form of currency in Duat. These can be earned in Duat if necessary. Good Deeds are positive actions which are helpful to others. Bad Deeds subtract from the score. Deeds are recorded by **Thoth** & his assistant, **Seshet**.

The offices of the Asmarians are their homes when not incarnate on Planets. The **Book of Time** is in Ptah's locked office. It is read by Cherubim (a form of Angel). The Book of Time is written events in Time, containing all the necessary pathways and choices per life. It also references entertainment, politics, wars, books, films, games, etc. on Earth.

Asmarians in Duat can communicate **via Telepathy** from those on Earth. Telepathy is developed from hard prayer; the word Pray is derived from the **Sun** God, Ra, spelled as Pra with a long "A" vowel. **Ra created Magic** and Prayer is a form of Magical ritual from Ancient Egypt. **Hard Prayer** uses mental projections as opposed to Soft Prayer with vocalizations or common speech (one's voice, not internal reading voice). **Telepathy** sends thoughts, ideas, energy, and images **via radio waves** created from the **Sun.**

Say or think: "Dua Ptah di ankh hotepw Maa'hru." This will attract Akhu and maybe some Asmarians to you. **Repeat as necessary.**

Dua = Adore, Praise, Hail

Di = given or to give

Ankh = Life, Mirror, Reflection

Hotepw = Offerings; (Hotep = Peace)

Maa'hru = True of voice, justified in truth, Success, or becomes real upon speaking.

With developed **Telepathy** one can **attract** objects, food, money or prosperity, and mental energy from a distance. The objects usually come from people who connect with the Telepathy, or are receptive to it. One can also **repel** danger, feral animals or people, and **heal with energy** from one's **Ka** form. The **Ka** is your psychic/mental energy or "aura." In Psychoanalysis it is the "Id" and in Native Hawaii it is called "Mana."

You can also communicate with **Asmarians** from rituals like burning incense outside or in an Egyptian Temple or other modern refuge. Asmarians like offerings (Compensation). They also like Civil Order, Righteous Conduct of the Living, Artwork, **working technology**, precious stone jewelry, golden treasures in their Marble Temples, and happy citizens.

Sundays are the best time to communicate as this day was established for that purpose. The **Month of July** is especially sacred to Ptah as Gaius Julius **Caesar** (an incarnation of Ptah). One can also pilgrimage **to Egypt** to communicate with the Asmarians.

Bibliography:

https://www.academia.edu/44103699/Eye_of_the_Pharaoh

The Flawed Emerald by Michael J. Costa ©1995, ISBN: 0-75965-956-7

The Templars and the Grail, Knights of the Quest, © Karen Ralls 2003, ISBN: 0-8356-0807-7

https://www.academia.edu/45423821/Inside_the_Great_Pyramid_of_Khufu

https://csueb.academia.edu/MikeCosta

https://www.academia.edu/49007052/The_Burial_of_King_Ay_KV62_

The Holy Bible – King James Version

An Ancient Egyptian Hieroglyphic Dictionary, **Volume 1 – 2**, (EA Wallis Budge), © Dover Publications

How to read Egyptian Hieroglyphs – a step-by-step guide to teach yourself © Mark Collier, Bill Manley, 1998 University of California Press, ISBN: 0-965-69303-1

The Complete Gods & Goddesses of Ancient Egypt © 2003 Richard H. Wilkinson (Thames & Hudson). ISBN: 0-500-05120-8

The Complete Temples of Ancient Egypt © Richard H. Wilkinson, 2000 T&H, ISBN: 0-500-05100-3.

The British Museum Book of Ancient Egypt, © Stephen Quirke & Jeffrey Spencer, 1992, ISBN: 0-500-27902-0

An Egyptian Priest Magicianary © Horus Michael, 2016. ISBN: 9781523606566.

Amulets of Ancient Egypt © Carol Andrews 1994, University of Texas Press, ISBN: 0-292-704640-X

Magic in Ancient Egypt © Geraldine Pinch, 1994 University of Texas Press, ISBN: 0-292-76559-2

The Ancient Egyptian Book of the Dead © R. O. Faulkner, 1997 University of Texas Press, ISBN: 0-292-7042509

The Discovery of the tomb of Tutankhamen by © Howard Carter.

The Ancient and Mystical Order Rosa Crux (AMORC); Rosicrucian Library

The Wordsworth Handbook of Kings & Queens by the Late Professor of History, John E. Morby (1939-2010); from CSUEB

Child Labor = The Children of God (in Bible).

https://www.theguardian.com/science/2017/jun/0
6/did-children-build-the-ancient-egyptian-city-of-
armana-

https://www.nationalgeographic.com/history/artic
le/130313-ancient-egypt-akhenaten-amarna-
cemetery-archaeology-science-world

https://enterprise.press/stories/2017/06/07/ancie
nt-egyptian-city-of-tell-el-amarna-built-by-child-
labor/

https://ehistory.osu.edu/biographies/amenhotep-
iv-akhenaton

https://www.britannica.com/biography/Akhenaten

https://en.wikipedia.org/wiki/Akhenaten

www.amazon.com/author/horusmichael

www.amazon.com/author/michaeljcosta

Hieroglyphic Font by **Inscribe**.

www.arce.org (The American Research Center in
Egypt)

https://www.imdb.com/title/tt1133985/

https://en.wikipedia.org/wiki/Green_Lantern

*Alan Scott's Green Lantern history originally began
thousands of years ago when a mystical "green
flame" meteor fell to Earth in ancient China.*

About the Author:

Pharaoh/Chief Lector Priest for the Internet Temple of Amon-Ra, **Horus Michael I** follows the training of Ancient Egyptian Priests in his varied works on the Occult. He also studies Egyptian Archaeology (**Egyptology**). www.arce.org

The Asmarians:

The Aliens Who Built the Egyptian Pyramids

What does Modern Egyptology know about the Egyptian Philosopher's Stone created with Alchemy, or its alien origins? The green Alien crystal that cut granite blocks like a diamond cuts through glass, was developed to build the Pyramids of Egypt, as copper tools didn't cut the stone blocks so precisely. What was the relationship between the Asmarian crystals and the Holy Grail? Who are the Asmarians?